15.95

W9-ASL-411

DATE DUE

15.95

The Hispanics

Greg Nickles

 CRABTREE
Publishing Company

CRABTREE
Publishing Company

PMB 16A 350 Fifth Avenue
Suite 3308
New York, NY 10118

612 Welland Avenue
St. Catharines, Ontario
L2M 5V6

Co-ordinating editor: Ellen Rodger
Content editor: Virginia Mainprize
Contributing Editor: Lisa Gurusinghe
Production co-ordinator: Rosie Gowsell
Cover design: Robert MacGregor

Film: Embassy Graphics

Printer: Worzalla Publishing Company

Created by: Brown Partworks Ltd
Commissioning editor: Anne O'Daly
Project editor: Caroline Beattie
Picture researcher: Adrian Bentley
Editorial assistant: Chris Wiegand
Maps: Mark Walker
Consultant: Professor Donald Avery

CATALOGING-IN-PUBLICATION DATA
Nickles, Greg, 1969-
    The Hispanics / Greg Nickles.– 1st ed.
    p.cm. – (We Came to North America)
    Includes index.
    ISBN 0-7787-0186-7 (RLB) –ISBN 0-7787-0200-6 (pbk.)
    1. Hispanic Americans–History–Juvenile literature.
2. United States–Civilization–Hispanic influences–Juvenile literature. 3. North America–Relations–Latin America–Juvenile literature. 4. Latin American–Relations–North America–Juvenile literature. [1. Hispanic Americans–History. 2. United States–Civilization–Hispanic influences. 3. North America–Relations–Latin America. 4. Latin America–Relations–North America.] I. Title. II Series.
    E184.S75 N53 2001
    973'.0468–dc21   00-043227
                    LC

Photographs
AKG London AP 15 (top); Evelyn Henn 30; Palacio de los Borbones, Escorial 6. **Corbis** 17, 31 (bottom); AFP/Jeff Kowalski 31(bottom); Bettmann 5 (bottom), 14, 21; David Robinson 23b; J. Sohm/ChromoSohm 28; Kelly-Mooney Photography front cover, 26 (bottom); Nik Wheeler 23 (above); Owen Franken 22, 25; Pablo Corral V 13 (bottom); Richard Cummins 29 (bottom); Robert van der Hilst 13 (above); Sandy Felsenthal 5 (top); Tony Arruza 18 (top), 29 (top);. **Hulton Getty** Ernst Haas 8 (bottom): **The Image Bank** Archive Photos 10, 19, 31 (top left). **Peter Newark's Pictures** 4 (bottom), 7(top), 8 (top), 9, 11 (top), 11 (bottom), back cover; **Sylvia Cordaiy Photo Library** Bjanka Kadic 4 (top); **Travel Ink** Abbie Enock 15 (bottom), 18 (bottom); Andrew Watson 26 (top); Simon Reddy 27. **Werner Forman Archive** National Museum of Anthropology, Mexico City 7 (bottom)

Cover: Mexican-American dancers celebrate their culture at a festival.

Book Credits
page 16: *Barrio Boy* by Ernesto Galarza. Published by University of Notre Dame Press. Reprinted by permission of the publisher.

page 20: *Tropic in Manhattan* by Guillermo Cotto-Thorner, originally published as *Tropico en Manhattan* by the Spanish-American Printing Co. in 1951. Quoted in *Who Built America?* Volume 2, American Social History Project, Pantheon, 1992.

page 24: *Out of the Ashes: The lives and hopes of refugees from El Salvador and Guatemala*, published by El Salvador and Guatemala Committees for Human Rights and WOW Campaigns Ltd.

Contents

Introduction

Hispanics are the **descendants** of Spanish-speaking peoples in North America. Some of their **ancestors** lived on the continent long before the countries of Canada and the United States were created. Others lived in the Caribbean and Latin America. They all share a long, proud history.

Hispanic peoples are very **diverse**. They have many different histories and **cultures** because they come from so many places. Most Hispanics are descendants of Spanish people and Native Americans, and some have African ancestors. Many use Spanish as their first language, but some do not speak Spanish at all, or have learned it as a second language in school.

Since 1980, the name "Hispanic" has been used by the United States government to describe all people of Spanish-speaking heritage. Many Hispanics accept this name, but not everyone likes it. Some choose the name "Latino" instead. Others, such as Cubans, Mexicans, Puerto Ricans, and Salvadorans, prefer names that show their place of origin.

▲ **New Yorkers of Dominican origins attend a rally in a park.**

▼ **The Spanish forced many Native Americans to become Catholics.**

Hispanics trace back part of their history over 500 years, to the time when explorers from Spain crossed the Atlantic Ocean to North, Central, and South America. The explorers were met by Native American peoples who had lived in these lands for thousands of years. The Spaniards brutally conquered many of these peoples and took over their lands. They set up a huge empire that stretched across the Americas.

Spanish settlers brought their language, religion, and culture with them. They introduced European-style governments, cities, and farms. As time passed, many children were born of Spanish and Native-American parents. By the time the United States and Canada were created in the 1700s and 1800s, Spanish settlements in the Americas had grown into many thriving Hispanic communities.

Some Hispanics, who lived in areas that today make up such states as California, Florida, and Texas, became citizens of the United States when it took over those lands. Millions more moved to the United States later, especially during the last half of the twentieth century. Some Hispanics settled in Canada. Most of these later **immigrants** were fleeing poverty, brutal governments, or wars in their home countries.

Hispanics and their descendants have made important contributions in many fields, such as science, politics, business, performing arts, and literature. However, Hispanics in North America have often faced **discrimination**. For years, they have fought for equal rights and fairer treatment. Although they have won many victories, Hispanics today continue to campaign for better jobs, housing, and education.

▲ Two girls show their pride in their country of origin by wearing Guatemalan clothes for a parade in Chicago.

► A group of Hispanic grape pickers led by Cesar Chavez, who fought for better working conditions for Hispanic farm workers.

Spain and the Americas

Hispanics are proud of their Spanish and Native-American ancestors, as well as their African ones. Each of these groups had ancient and rich cultures before 1492, the year in which Christopher Columbus first sailed from Spain to the Americas.

In 1492, people were only beginning to learn about the world. Before Christopher Columbus's voyage, few Europeans knew that the Americas existed. Native Americans also did not know about the world's other continents, peoples, and cultures.

In those days, Spain was a strong kingdom. It had a fleet of many sailing ships and a large, well-trained army. Like other European countries, Spain was ruled by a royal family and was often at war with other countries, such as England, France, and Portugal. The rulers fought to take over each other's lands and make their own country the most powerful in Europe.

▲ A map of Spain around 1492.

◄ In 1492, the Moors, who had ruled much of Spain for centuries, were defeated by the Spanish.

Christopher Columbus

In 1492, Italian explorer Christopher Columbus led an expedition, paid for by the king and queen of Spain, that discovered a sea route from Europe to the Americas. Columbus landed in the Caribbean, but he was actually looking for a route to India, China, and Japan. Europeans called these faraway Asian lands the Indies and thought they were filled with gold and other treasures. At the time, no one knew that the Americas and the Pacific Ocean lay between Europe and Asia's eastern shore. Although Columbus was not the first European to set foot in this so-called "New World" (Vikings had visited the coast of Canada about 500 years before), his discovery led the way for Europeans to explore, conquer, and settle there.

▲ **Columbus says goodbye to Queen Isabella and King Ferdinand before crossing the Atlantic Ocean.**

The Spaniards were members of the Roman Catholic Church. This church is part of the Christian religion, which worships Jesus Christ and follows the teachings of the Bible. In addition to wanting new lands and riches for their country, the Spaniards felt it was their duty to **convert** other people and make them accept Christian beliefs.

Across the Atlantic Ocean, Native Americans had very different traditions than the Spaniards'. The hundreds of Native American **civilizations** each had its own rich culture, history, and way of life. A few, such as the Aztec, Maya, and Inca, had wealthy empires with powerful armies, large cities, and well-organized governments. Other Native Americans lived in smaller towns or villages, and still others were nomads who followed herds of animals and hunted for food and hides. Although these communities had different languages and cultures, they shared a respect for family life, traded with other tribes, and worshiped the great gods and spirits of nature.

◀ **A gold pendant made by the Mixtec, who lived in Mexico before the arrival of the Spanish.**

Journeys to North America

Following the historic voyage of Columbus, the Spaniards made many other trips to the Americas. They hoped to find gold and silver and new lands to claim for their country, as well as a sea route to the Indies. In those days, sailing trips, especially into the unmapped Atlantic and Pacific Oceans, were very dangerous.

Many ships were lost in storms at sea, or their crews died far from home of starvation or disease. Ships were so small and packed with supplies that sailors had to sleep on deck. Day after day, they struggled to fight off boredom as they did the same chores, wore the same clothes, and ate the same dried foods.

The Spaniards' desire to explore and find treasure outweighed the dangers of sailing. After they conquered the Caribbean, the Spaniards sailed along the Atlantic coasts of North, Central, and South America. On Easter Sunday in 1513, Juan Ponce de León landed along what is now the United States mainland.

▲ Juan Ponce de León fighting with Native Americans.

◄ This drawing, on the wall in the Canyon de Chelly in Arizona, is thought to show the invasion of North America by the Spaniards, as it shows a Christian cross.

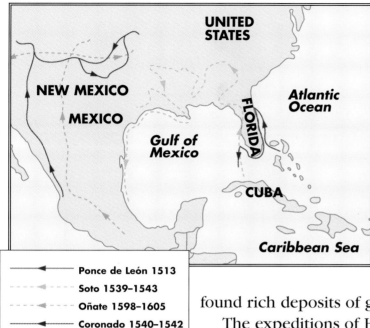

Juan Ponce de León claimed the area for Spain. He named it "La Florida" for its beautiful flowers and for the Easter holiday, which in Spanish is *Pascua florida*. La Florida was a huge territory that included the future state of Florida, as well as the lands west to Texas.

Within a few years, Spanish expeditions sailed along the coasts of the Gulf of Mexico and the Atlantic. No sea route to Asia was discovered. The Spaniards instead found rich deposits of gold and silver.

The expeditions of Hernando de Soto in 1539, Francisco Vásquez de Coronado in 1540, and Juan de Oñate in 1601 explored the south and southwest of what is today the United States. Along the way, these explorers claimed vast lands for Spain, opening the door for thousands of Spaniards to settle there.

▲ Explorers' journeys in what are now Mexico and the United States.

Map legend:
- Ponce de León 1513
- Soto 1539–1543
- Oñate 1598–1605
- Coronado 1540–1542

The Spanish Conquest

The meeting between the peoples of Spain and the Americas caused terrible hardships for Native Americans. The Spaniards took over their lands, forcing thousands to adopt Spanish customs and work as slaves. Native Americans also caught deadly diseases, such as smallpox, that Europeans unknowingly carried. These diseases killed millions of people.

Where the Native Americans would not cooperate, they were brutally conquered by soldiers. The most famous Spanish conquerors, or conquistadors, were Hernán Cortés and Francisco Pizarro. In 1521, with the help of other Native Americans who wanted to get rid of the powerful Aztecs, Cortés destroyed the Aztecs' mighty empire in Mexico. In the 1530s, Pizarro took advantage of a local civil war to crush the huge South American empire of the Incas.

▲ Cortés, on horseback, in battle against the Aztecs of Mexico.

Early Settlements in North America

After the Native Americans had been conquered, the Spanish established settlements throughout their empire. At first, they came because of the rich supplies of gold and silver. Later, they set up huge plantations and ranches. They forced hundreds of thousands of Native Americans to work as slaves.

Once their first settlements were established in the Caribbean and Mexico in the early 1500s, the Spaniards turned to the lands that today make up the southern and southwestern United States. In 1565, Spanish Admiral Pedro Menéndez de Avilés founded the outpost of San Augustín (now Saint Augustine) in La Florida. It soon became the capital of the region which included many small towns, *presidios*, or forts, and large cattle ranches.

In the following years, Spaniards built bases along the Atlantic coast as far north as the Carolinas and west around the Gulf of Mexico. During the 1600s and 1700s, settlements were also founded throughout Spanish territories in Texas, California, and the southwest. At the height of their success, these communities bustled with activity.

▲ Saint Augustine in 1671. It is today one of the oldest surviving European settlements in North America.

Spanish Missions

Roman Catholic settlements, called missions, played a key role in settling Spain's empire. They were run by *padres* (priests) who believed it was their duty to convert Native Americans to Christianity and teach them European ways. *Padres* made Native Americans abandon their traditional language, customs, and religion and taught them Spanish and European skills such as leatherworking, cattle ranching, and carpentry.

▲ A Spanish mission in California in 1830, when it was part of Mexico.

Traders bought and sold goods, artisans crafted their wares, herders rounded up livestock, and Roman Catholic priests looked after the religious needs of the settlers. Some settler families came, but most newcomers were single men who hoped to earn a living, then start a family in the Americas or return rich to Spain. Some settlements failed because they did not have enough food or supplies. Others were attacked by local Native Americans in **retaliation** for the brutal way in which they were treated by the Spanish. Most of the settlements in La Florida were wiped out by French and British forces in the early 1700s.

In the early 1800s, the growing United States took over La Florida. By the mid-1800s, after a war between Mexico and the United States, much of Mexico's northern lands, including California, the southwest, and Texas, were also taken over by the United States. These changes caused great hardships in the Hispanic settlements. Hispanic people found themselves outnumbered by English-speaking settlers, ranchers, and miners, who often took away their farms, businesses, and homes.

▼ A *vaquero* (cowboy) brands a steer in Spanish California in the 1850s.

Latin America

Most Hispanics in the United States and Canada today have their roots in Latin America. Latin America is made up of many countries in the Caribbean and North, Central, and South America where Spanish is the main language.

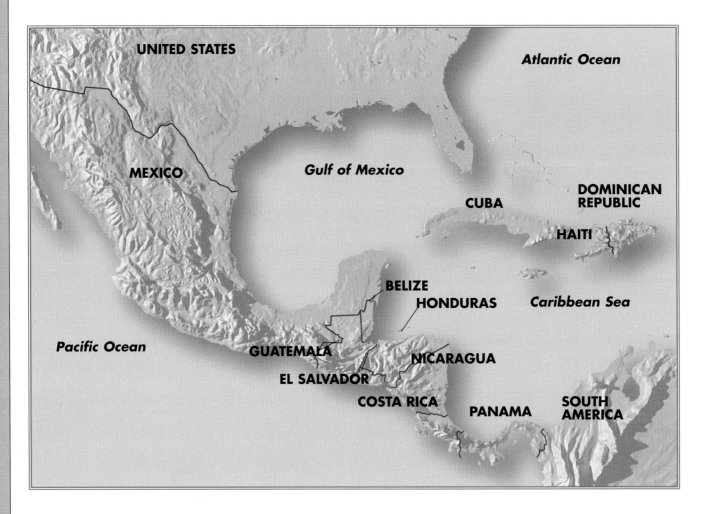

Today, many of the customs and beliefs practiced throughout Latin America reflect different Spanish, Native American, and African traditions. Spaniards from different regions in Spain brought their customs and religion to the Americas. Native Americans also passed on their traditions to their Hispanic descendants. In the Caribbean, where the Spaniards wiped out most Native Americans through disease, overwork, and war, Hispanic cultures were strongly influenced by African slaves brought there by the Europeans.

▲ **Most Hispanics in the United States come from Central America and the Caribbean countries.**

Both Worlds

The main religion throughout Latin America is Christianity, introduced by the Spaniards. Most of their Native American and African subjects adopted Roman Catholic beliefs but often continued to celebrate their own ancient religions, blending them with Christianity. In the African-based religion called Santeria, for example, people substitute Roman Catholic **saints** for their ancient gods.

▲ A shrine in a house in Cuba is dedicated to a Santeria saint.

Hispanics in Latin America also have different histories. Some have found peace and success in their countries, but many have been troubled by violence and poverty. For example, Puerto Rico has enjoyed political **stability** since it became part of the United States in 1898. Both Cuba and Mexico, however, have had corrupt rulers and bloody revolutions in the last century. Hispanics in the Dominican Republic suffered for 30 years under a brutal leader, and in parts of South America, governments **persecuted** some of their citizens.

▼ A Venezuelan family works together sorting coffee beans.

Throughout Latin America today, many people, especially in the countryside, live in poverty and have difficulty getting a good education or finding jobs. There is some office and manufacturing work, and sometimes jobs in tourism, but people often must work long hours for low wages. Many are farmers who struggle to grow enough food for their families. There are also some very wealthy, successful people who hold jobs in government or professions such as medicine and business.

Whatever their background, people in Latin America most often look to Canada and the United States as places to escape whatever difficulties they face in their own countries. Those who **emigrate** usually come in seach of a higher standard of living and better education, work, and health care.

The Journey from Latin America

Latin Americans have moved to the United States and Canada at many times and for different reasons. Most came to build a new life. Others planned to stay only until the political situation in their own countries improved and they could safely return home. Some came to earn extra money as migrant workers.

People of Mexican heritage make up the largest group of Hispanics in the United States. Many thousands became U.S. citizens in the 1800s, when the United States took over the Mexican lands of Texas, the southwest, and California. Since the Mexican Revolution in 1910, millions have moved north from Mexico to find work and escape their country's political and economic troubles. Despite the **controversy** over illegal border crossings, Mexican immigrants are an important **asset** to the U.S. economy. Some have jobs as **migrant** farm workers, others live in the cities of the United States and Canada.

▲ The areas in the United States and Canada where most Hispanics have settled.

◄ Puerto Ricans hold a protest march to demand improvements in education in New York City.

A Long Road

Hispanics immigrants who speak only Spanish or have little education often find it hard to get good jobs in their new lands. Many have to settle for unskilled or part-time work, low wages, and run-down housing. They have fewer opportunities for better jobs, education, or to improve their standard of living. Nevertheless, thousands of Hispanics come each year to North America, both legally and in secret, hoping for a better life.

▲ **Refugees from Cuba, crowded into a small boat, wait for the arrival of an immigration officer so that they can go ashore in Florida.**

▼ **Some Hispanics run shops in North America which are very useful for Hispanics who do not speak English.**

Puerto Ricans make up the second-largest Hispanic group in the United States. Because Puerto Rico is part of the United States, people who live there are U.S. citizens. In the last century, hundreds of thousands of poverty-weary Puerto Ricans have moved to New York and other major cities in search of better lives. Most have come since the 1940s, when airplanes made the journey shorter and easier than by boat.

Most Cuban Americans, who make up America's third-largest Hispanic group, have moved to the United States, to Miami, Florida, in particular, as **refugees** since the 1950s. They came fleeing political and economic problems at home.

Dominicans are among the latest Hispanic immigrants. Most have come since the 1960s to escape political violence. Today, they continue to leave the Dominican Republic by the thousands in search of work, settling mainly in New York, Miami, and other eastern cities. Those who can afford to buy a ticket fly to the mainland United States. Others dare a risky sea voyage to Puerto Rico and travel secretly to other parts of the United States.

Although immigrants from South America are few compared to other Hispanics in North America, they make up a diverse and important group. Some, such as the Chilean political refugees who moved to Canada in the 1970s, fled from their countries. Others left to make a better life for themselves. Most South Americans have moved to New York, Chicago, San Francisco, and Montréal.

Eyewitness to History

ERNESTO GALARZA grew up in a mountain village in central Mexico. He and his family were forced to leave their village because of the Mexican Revolution in 1910. They drifted from town to town in Mexico and then traveled across the border to Tucson, Arizona. They settled finally in Sacramento, California. In this passage from his autobiography, *Barrio Boy*, Galarza describes the life of the *chicanos,* unskilled workers who arrived in the United States from Mexico.

" As poor refugees, their first concern was to find a place to sleep, then to eat and find work. In the *barrio* they were most likely to find all three, for not knowing English, they needed something that was even more urgent than a room, a meal, or a job, and that was information in a language they could understand. This information had to be picked up in bits and pieces — from families like ours, from the conversation groups in the poolrooms and the saloons.

Beds and meals, if the newcomers had no money at all, were provided — in one way or another — on trust, until the new *chicano* found a job. On trust and not on credit, for trust was something between people who had plenty of nothing, and credit was between people who had something of plenty. It was not charity or social welfare but something my mother called *asistencia*, a helping given and received on trust, to be repaid because those who had given it were themselves in need of what they had given. *Chicanos* who had found work on farms or in railroad camps came back to pay us a few dollars for *asistencia* we had provided weeks or months before. "

First Impressions: Miami

Many Hispanics, especially Cubans, have moved to Florida. In Miami, Cubans have built a community that looks and feels so much like their home country that it has been called "Little Havana," after Havana, Cuba's capital city.

Florida has been linked to Latin America since the days of Spain's empire. In the early 1800s, Florida was **annexed** by the United States, and by the 1900s, it had become a U.S. state. Some Cuban families lived there, mostly working in the cigar-making industry. Others came to escape the **corrupt** government in their homeland.

▲ A Cuban market stand in Little Havana, Miami, with Cuban products and magazines in Spanish.

In the late 1950s and early 1960s, hundreds of thousands of new Cuban refugees came to the United States after a revolution swept through their country. Cuba's new government was **communist** and did not allow people to own businesses or property, or to express their ideas freely. The United States government opposed communism. It encouraged Cubans to come to the United States, offering job training, English instruction, and other special services. Miami, with its beaches and palm trees was their favorite place to settle.

▶ An outside mural in Ybor City, the Cuban area of Tampa, Florida, shows women making cigars.

Many of the immigrants had excellent business skills, and a good education. Their aim was to recreate the comfortable lives they had left behind in Cuba. They set to work making the neighborhood in Miami look and feel as much like Cuba as possible. They renovated buildings and established new Cuban-style shops, restaurants, clubs, movie theaters, and other businesses. Spanish became the main language on signs and in conversation on the street. Little Havana — a community where Cubans could live almost as if they had never left their home country — was born.

The community's success in Miami, compared with Cuba's economic problems, attracted later waves of refugees in 1980 and again in the 1990s. These Cuban immigrants were mainly **working-class** and impoverished people fleeing their country and hoping for a better life in the United States. Often lacking the money, skills, and education of the first refugees, they have had a harder time finding success in Little Havana.

Today, Miami is home to hundreds of thousands of Cuban Americans and continues to thrive. Little Havana is now a popular attraction for tourists from all over the world, who come to enjoy the Cuban atmosphere. The neighborhood is changing, however. Other Hispanic peoples, such as Nicaraguans, have moved to the area, while many young Cuban Americans who have become successful and **prosperous** have moved away from Little Havana to Miami's suburbs.

Longing for Home

Although they were so successful in the United States, many Cuban immigrants hoped that Cuba's government would fall and that they could return to their country one day. As the **decades** passed, the communist government stayed in power, and the immigrants grew older. Today, their children and grandchildren, raised in the United States, think of themselves as Cuban American and have no desire to move to their parents' island home.

▲ **Older members of the Cuban community in Miami play dominoes.**

Eyewitness to History

GUILLERMO COTTO-THORNER came to New York City as an immigrant in the 1940s. Here, in his novel *Tropic in Manhattan*, he describes the Puerto Rican section of New York City.

" Juan Marcos had read and heard so much about El Barrio, the Puerto Rican colony in Manhattan scattered all over lower Harlem. Leaving the subway station, he stopped instinctively to look it over…. On both sides of the wide street, [he] could only distinguish two large buildings which stretched from corner to corner. Parallel windows, identical stairs reaching down to the sidewalk from six floors above the street. No, they weren't two buildings: they were many apartment buildings stuck together…. Hundreds, thousands of fellow Puerto Ricans lived there who, like him, had left the island to try their luck in New York….

Two men were playing checkers on a little table they had brought out onto the sidewalk, while two others watched. They were in front of 'The Cave,' a Puerto Rican 'greasy spoon,' which exuded the delicious aromas of fried pork rinds, *pasteles*, and fried codfish….

'This,' [said] Antonio, 'is our neighborhood, El Barrio. It's said that we Latins run things here. And that's how we see ourselves. While the Americans take most of the money that circulates around here, we consider this part of the city to be ours…. The stores, barbershops, restaurants, butcher shops, churches, funeral parlors, greasy spoons, pool halls, everything is all Latino. Every now and then you see a business run by a Jew or an Irishman or an Italian, but you'll also see that even these people know a little Spanish. "

Refugees from Central America

Many of the latest Hispanic immigrants to the United States and Canada have come from Central American countries, mainly El Salvador, Nicaragua, and Guatemala. Some of these peoples moved to escape poverty, but many others were forced to flee their homes as refugees, fearing for their lives.

Central America is the area of land that links the continents of North and South America. Under Spanish rule, this **fertile** region was used as farmland for growing crops. In the 1800s, control of Central America passed briefly to Mexico from Spain before the local peoples won their independence and established their own small countries.

For years, the peoples of Central America were ruled by many unfair and harsh governments. Few people left their countries, however, until severe troubles broke out in the late 1970s. In both El Salvador and Nicaragua, small bands of rebel fighters, called guerrillas, began wars against their brutal governments. In Guatemala in 1982, the government was taken over by military leaders. In the terrible years that followed in these countries, hundreds of thousands of people were murdered by soldiers, and millions more were made homeless.

Refugees flooded across the borders seeking safety in neighboring countries. Many of the refugees were put into crowded, dirty camps in these border countries where they waited until it was safe to go home.

▲ **In El Salvador, armed fighters pose for a moment in front of a police station they have just destroyed.**

Pitfalls along the Way

Getting to the United States and Canada has been a difficult and sometimes dangerous journey for many Central-American refugees. They traveled through other Central-American countries and Mexico to reach the southern border of the United States. Many ended up in refugee camps along the way. Some were rescued by church

▲ **Refugees from El Salvador living in Los Angeles attend a crowded meeting.**

groups from the United States and Canada, which helped them across the borders and to rebuild their lives. Like many other Hispanic immigrants, Central Americans have moved mostly to large cities. Most Nicaraguans settled in Miami, Florida. Los Angeles, California, has become such a popular **destination** for Central Americans, especially El Salvadorans and Guatemalans, that some people now call it the Central-American capital of the United States. Canada has also accepted tens of thousands of Central Americans, many of whom now live in Toronto and Montréal.

▼ **Posters criticizing U.S. involvement in the wars in Nicaragua and in El Salvador.**

By the early 1990s, when most of the violence had stopped, El Salvador, Nicaragua, and Guatemala were in **shambles**. Towns, farms, and roads were destroyed, and people could no longer earn their living. Since the wars, many thousands of Central Americans have continued to leave their countries to escape poverty.

Eyewitness to History

This account by a Salvadoran child living in a refugee camp tells of the terrors from which some refugees were escaping.

" I'm eleven years old and I used to live in a village called Mozote. Well, what happened was that the armed forces arrived in 1981. They were everywhere. They slept the night in Mozote. Then at around ten in the morning the soldiers went to all the houses and said that they'd give us a present if we went into the square. When everybody had come into the square they made us line up; one line of old people, one of young and one of the little ones. There were already a few people locked in the church. They put four gunmen in the church, one in each doorway. Then they began to shoot the people in the church and those in the lines in the square. When they'd killed the old people they began to kill the young. Well, there were only three of us left, so I ran for it. I ran until I reached Los Toriles. When I got there there was another column of soldiers. As they passed I hid. When I arrived in the village all the people there were dead. I ran into the woods and when I saw that they were setting fire to all the houses I went on further. There, they were also burning houses and killing people. So when I saw that there were no people there either, I ran and hid in a cave. I stayed there during the daytime. When I was in the cave I didn't have anything to eat. I couldn't go out because I could still hear the shooting. So I only went out at night. I was all alone there. My mother and father and my eight brothers and sisters had all been killed in Mozote. "

Culture and Traditions

Hispanics celebrate a rich variety of customs and traditions. They brought some from Latin America and invented others in their new homes. For hundreds of years, Hispanic cultures have had an important influence on the culture of North America.

ispanic culture is rich in music, which is usually paired with exciting dances. This music has roots in sounds brought from Africa and Spain, which then **evolved** in each Latin America and Caribbean country. Rumba, tango, conga, mambo, cha-cha, and merengue are just a few of the energetic styles of music and dance that became popular in the twentieth century. Hispanic rhythms have also strongly influenced other music styles, such as jazz, rock, and country music. Today, punchy salsa music, the light pop of the "Miami sound," and tejano, which is rooted in traditional folk songs, are some of the styles most popular with Hispanics and other North Americans.

▲ A Spanish mission church in Tucson, Arizona. This style of building blended with local styles to produce modern Hispanic architecture.

◄ Mexican traditions of music and dance are alive and well in a street festival in Austin, Texas.

From Spanish to English

Today, the English language owes hundreds of its words to Spanish. Most were words adopted by English-speaking peoples who met Hispanics in North America. Some words, such as *adios*, *amigo*, *cafetería*, *mosquito*, and *sombrero*, are exactly the same as in Spanish, but others, such as those listed below, have been adapted into English.

English	Spanish
alligator	from *el lagarto*, "the lizard"
cockroach	from *cucaracha*
tornado	from *tronada*, "thunderstorm"
stampede	from *estampida*

Thousands of place names, including states such as California, Montana, and Texas, and the cities of Los Angeles, San Francisco, and Las Vegas, also are Spanish in origin.

The same variety as in music and dance is found in Hispanic **cuisine**. Mexican food, now served in restaurants and homes across the continent, is known for its hot, spicy flavors. Dishes include light fare, such as nachos, tacos, and tortillas, and heavier burritos and chili. Few people know that chocolate came from the Native Americans of ancient Mexico, who drank it mixed with hot chiles. Today, both cocoa and the more than 100 varieties of chile peppers are main ingredients in Mexican cooking.

Basic Puerto Rican dishes are often made of chicken or beans with rice. Tasty sweets, such as *pirulis*, or sugar sticks, are a favorite. Cuban foods also feature rice and beans, as well as delicious soups and *yuca*, a root vegetable.

Hispanic architecture and art have a long history in North America. The centuries-old architecture of Spanish missions and forts, in Texas, the southwest, and California, lives on in the design of many modern homes. One of the most traditional styles of art is the painting of beautiful *santos*, or religious portraits, on wood panels for churches. **Mural** painting is a younger tradition from Mexico, used in the 1960s and 1970s by Mexican-American artists to promote Hispanic pride. On walls throughout Hispanic neighborhoods, colorful murals show scenes from their community's history.

▼ A Mexican meal mixes textures, colors, and flavors.

Fiestas

Throughout the year, Hispanic families all over North America gather to celebrate special days, from birthdays to fiestas, or festivals. No celebration is complete without brightly colored flowers and decorations, delicious food, and plenty of music and dancing.

Festivals, especially those on Roman Catholic holy days, are celebrated by many Hispanic peoples. Each community also has its own fiestas, which remember national holidays or saints of its home country. Sporting events, the birthdays of famous Hispanics, and traditional Native-American rituals, such as those that are meant to encourage good crops, are also reason for celebration. In New York, Miami, Los Angeles, and other large cities, many fiestas have become large parties joined by people from all backgrounds.

Among the most popular celebrations in the Cuban community are *quinceañeras*. A *quinceañera* is a party that celebrates a girl's fifteenth birthday. The day often begins with a religious service at church. The young woman may wear a traditional white gown and be attended by up to fourteen of her female friends. Later, she is the guest of honor at a grand dinner and dance.

▲ **Puerto Ricans holding flags are part of a parade in Wilmington, Delaware.**

Piñatas

Animal-shaped *piñatas*, a traditional favorite of Mexican families, are popular at children's parties all over North America. They are made from brightly decorated paper or clay and filled with candies, fruits, and small toys. A *piñata* is hung from a tree or from the ceiling, and struck with a stick by blindfolded children. When the *piñata* is finally broken open, the treats inside spill to the ground, and everyone scrambles to scoop up as many as possible.

◄ **Children at a party all take turns to hit the *piñata* to get at all the candies and toys.**

One of the largest Mexican fiestas is *el día de los muertos*, the Day of the Dead. It is held over the first two days of November, when legend says the spirits of dead people return to visit the living. Families hang paper skeletons in their homes and decorate foods, flags, and clothing with skull-and-bone patterns. Some people build a shrine in their home with photos and belongings of their dead loved ones. On November 1, people join in a procession to the cemetery, where they tidy relatives' graves and leave offerings of candles, food, and flowers.

The largest Puerto Rican fiesta is the Feast of San Juan, Puerto Rico's official saint, on June 24. On the nearest Sunday, the great Puerto Rican Day Parade is held in New York City. Huge crowds turn out to cheer the colorful floats, marching bands, and carnival dancers.

Of the Christian fiestas celebrated by Hispanics, *las Navidades* (Christmas) is especially festive. From mid-December until early January, friends and relatives pay surprise visits and throw parties. Christmas Eve is the day on which most families gather for a huge feast and midnight service at church. Epiphany, on January 6, is often the day when children receive presents, to remember that Jesus received gifts from the three kings on that day.

▼ **Wall decorations to celebrate the Day of the Dead in Los Angeles.**

DIA DE LOS MUERTOS NOV. 2

Hispanic Heroes

Building a new life in North America has been a challenge for many Hispanic immigrants and their descendants. They have been helped in their fight against discrimination and poverty by organizations created by fellow Hispanics. They have also found inspiration in Hispanics who have contributed to their communities.

In their fight to improve the daily lives of the people in their communities, many Hispanics in the United States have run for government office or formed political organizations. Throughout the mid-1900s, Hispanic politicians, such as U.S. Senators Dennis Chávez and Joseph M. Montoya, were a strong voice for their people. In the 1960s, Rodolfo "Corky" Gonzáles, Dolores Fernández Huerta, and thousands of other Hispanics joined the civil rights movement to end racial discrimination.

Their efforts won them Spanish-language programs in schools and fairer treatment in public and the workplace. They also helped to create a strong sense of Hispanic pride throughout the country.

▲ **Dolores Fernández Huerta, in a mural on Los Angeles' First Street Bridge by Yreina D. Cervantez. Huerta helped form the United Farm Workers of America and works to promote civil rights.**

▲ Husband and wife Desi Arnaz and Lucille Ball in their popular television show from the 1950s, *I Love Lucy*.

Hispanics have also become very important in the entertainment industry. Walt Disney, the creator of Mickey Mouse, was of Spanish-speaking ancestry, as was Desi Arnaz, the Cuban producer and co-star of the most popular television show of all time, *I Love Lucy*. Hispanic film and television stars include Martin Sheen, Raquel Welch, Jimmy Smits, Rosie Pérez, Andy García, Sally Jessy Raphaël, and Geraldo Rivera. The tradition of popular Hispanic musicians is today continued by such superstars as Gloria Estefan, Jennifer Lopez, Linda Ronstadt, Carlos Santana, and Ricky Martin. The 1989 Pulitzer Prize for Literature awarded to Oscar Hijuelos for his novel *The Mambo Kings Play Songs of Love* helped Hispanic voices gain much-deserved respect. It was the first such prize awarded to a Hispanic author.

The NASA space shuttle flights of Ellen Ochoa and Sidney M. Gutiérrez have helped recognize the value of Hispanics in science. Many Hispanics are also well known in sports, especially soccer, golf, and baseball. Juan "Chi Chi" Rodriguez and Nancy López are among today's biggest golf stars. Roberto Walker Clemente was one of baseball's all-time greats and a Hispanic hero. Respected for his views against discrimination, he died in a 1972 plane crash on his way to help earthquake victims in Nicaragua.

Justice in the Fields

Cesar E. Chavez was a hero to thousands of American farm workers. Born in 1927 in Arizona, he lived on his family's small farm until his father lost the land during the Depression. Chavez began working as a migrant farm worker at the age of 10. Migrant farm workers, many of whom were Mexican-American, worked long hours for little pay and could barely afford to feed themselves. Chavez's experiences with the poverty and inequality these people suffered made him decide to do something to better the lives of all farm workers. In the 1960s, he began organizing farm workers into a **union**. The United Farm Workers of America union helped migrant workers gain better pay and working conditions by fighting tough agriculture companies. Chavez died in 1993.

▲ Cesar Chavez fought for fair working conditions for farm workers.

Glossary

ancestor Family member from the past, such as a great-grandfather.

annex To add someone's land to one's own property.

asset Something of value.

civilization A highly developed state or society.

communist State control of all industry, property, and agriculture.

controversy Something causing a lot of debate and argument.

convert To change from one religion to another.

corrupt Dishonest.

culture A group of people's way of life, including their language, beliefs, and art.

cuisine Style of cooking.

decade A period of ten years.

descendant A family member such as a child, grandchild, and their children.

destination Place to which travelers are trying to get.

discrimination Unfair treatment of people because of their race, color, or religion.

diverse Different, varied.

emigrate To leave a country and make a new life in another country.

evolve To develop gradually.

fertile Producing good crops.

immigrant Someone who comes to settle in one country from another.

migrant Moving from one place to another.

mural Painting on a wall.

persecute To treat cruelly.

prosperous Successful.

retaliation The paying back of someone for an unkind act

refugee Someone who has to leave their own country for fear of war and other danger.

saint A holy person.

shambles Something that is confused and totally disorganized.

stability A safe and organized situation.

union A group of workers in a particular industry who fight for the best working conditions for their colleagues.

working-class A group of people in society who do not own much property and do physical work.

Index